the guide to owning a
Quaker Parrot

Gayle Soucek

Contents

Although prolific populations of feral Quakers have caused the species to be restricted in several states, most find the little birds to be harmless and enjoyable pets.

Introduction to Quaker Parrots

Often I'm asked which species of parrot will make a good "first bird," and invariably I find myself mentioning the Quaker. Quaker parrots, which are also known as Monk parakeets, are the sole members of the genus *Myiopsitta*. Four subspecies have been classified: the nominate *Myiopsitta monachus monachus*, *M.m. calita*, *M.m.cotorra*, and the rare and lesser-known *M.m.luchsi*. Quakers are South American parrots that range approximately from central Bolivia and southern Brazil down through parts of Argentina, primarily in lowland forests, although *M.m.luchsi* is found at higher altitudes and is known to nest on cliffs.

Quakers have also established feral communities in many places around the world, including Puerto Rico, Austria, Germany, and several locations throughout the Mediterranean and in the United States. In the Chicago area where I live we have enough feral populations dotting the city and suburbs that they've been included in local field guides to area birds. Chicago's late Mayor Harold Washington considered the little green parrots good luck charms, and a sizeable population in the city has remained carefully protected by local residents.

Before importation of wild parrots was stopped in the early 1990s, huge numbers of these birds were brought into the United States. During the seven-year period from 1983 through 1989, more than 308,000 Quakers were imported into the United States alone, ranking it the fourth most imported parrot species. It's easy to understand their charm. They are sturdy little birds with an expansive personality. Although they measure only about 11 inches from head to tail, most Quakers *think* they're much bigger. They're gregarious, inquisitive, aggressive, and they possess a strong talent for learning to talk. Properly socialized and raised with loving discipline, a Quaker can be a dream bird, one of the best companions you could ever hope to find. Unfortunately, a poorly trained and neglected Quaker can turn into a screaming, biting, angry little monster.

Quakers, in fact, tend to be one of the most loved *and* one of the most reviled birds in parrotdom. Because they are usually such delightful pets, Quaker owners and breeders are some of the most loyal fans of the species you'll ever meet. On the other hand, due to fears (mostly unfounded) that the feral populations in the U.S. will expand and become major crop threats, an anti-Quaker hysteria has descended on the lawmakers in some states. To date, seven states (California, Hawaii, Kentucky, Pennsylvania, Rhode Island, Tennessee, and Wyoming) have completely banned the trade, sale, or ownership of Quakers. Several others have laws on the books that put certain restrictions on sale or ownership, but these vary widely in interpretation and enforcement. If you have questions, you can call your state's Fish and Wildlife Department, but don't be surprised if the information you receive is vague or contradictory. In truth, many states don't really enforce these

The curious and sometimes aggressive Quaker does best in a household where it can be properly socialized and trained.

THE GUIDE TO OWNING A QUAKER PARROT

laws, and many "renegade" pets may exist. In contrast, Pennsylvania will seize and euthanize Quakers.

In general, if you find that breeders and shops in your state are openly selling the birds, then you don't have to worry. If you intend to buy one in another state, however, be very careful to check legality before you attempt to bring your pet home.

The whole issue of parrots as a crop threat is not new to the United States. In the 1800s, huge flocks of Carolina parakeets blanketed the skies of the eastern U.S. until they were hunted to extinction in the early part of the 1900s. The last known specimen died at the Cincinnati Zoo in 1918. Some people fear that the Quaker will exploit the niche vacated by the Carolina parakeet, but I believe that's impossible. For one thing, persecution by farmers wasn't the only factor that led to the extinction. As large numbers of settlers pushed westward across the country, huge tracts of forest were felled to make way for farmland. While this temporarily increased the food supply for the birds, valuable nesting sites disappeared and the population began to shrink. Soon, wide-scale hunting began, and the already threatened species vanished forever. As the character of the land itself changes, the type and number of species that the land can sustain also will change. This long-ignored lesson is being replayed all over the world today, as more and more species are threatened with extinction due to habitat destruction.

It is true that Quakers have some unique characteristics that make them more able

Quakers, also known as Monk parakeets, have great potential for training; some may even learn to talk.

to withstand environmental pressures. Unlike other parrots, which nest primarily in hollowed out tree cavities, Quakers build large, elaborate communal nests from sticks and twigs. Though they prefer to place these nests in trees, the always-adaptable Quaker is happy to use utility poles when a proper tree isn't handy. These nests can reach 20 feet across and hold dozens of individual birds. Each mated pair has its own private chamber, and the nests tend to be works-in-progress: new additions are added as needed. When the nest is destroyed by an act of nature or by a utility company miffed about shorted-out transformers, the birds simply start building all over again. When a large nest

Thanks to some unusual nesting and survival skills, the South American Quaker has been able to thrive in northern urban environments.

built atop power lines in a nearby Chicago suburb began causing fires and had to be removed, a local photographer captured a poignant scene. As the utility company workers picked the final bits of nest from around the transformer, a lone Quaker sat patiently on a nearby wire with a twig in his mouth, waiting for the intruders to leave so that he could get to work rebuilding.

It's these specialized nests and the indomitable spirit of these little green and gray parrots that helps them to survive even our harsh northern winters. It's that spirit that also makes them such attractive companions.

THE GUIDE TO OWNING A QUAKER PARROT

Buying a Pet Quaker

Once you've made the decision to add a Quaker parrot to your household, you'll want to do some homework to make sure you get a bird that is healthy and well socialized. A parrot (or any other pet, for that matter) should never be an impulse purchase. Parrots are extremely long-lived creatures, and they bond very

Like any other bird, the decision to buy a Quaker should not be taken lightly; Quakers require long-term care and commitment.

A recently weaned handfed baby is often the preferred choice for many owners, but an older, already trained Quaker may also be a good match.

HANDFED BABIES

Your best bet for a tame pet (especially if this is your first bird) is a recently weaned, handfed baby. Parrot chicks are altricial, which means that the baby is hatched blind, naked, and helpless, and needs to be fed and warmed by the parents for many weeks or months until it is able to survive on its own. To create a very tame, trusting bird, most parrot breeders remove the chicks from the nest while they are still helpless and take over the duties of the parent birds. These chicks (called "handfed" in the pet trade) lose all fear of humans and make excellent pets. Quakers wean and are able to eat on their own at about 8 to 12 weeks, and this is a perfect time for them to go to a new loving home.

You may be tempted to save money by buying a Quaker that is not yet weaned and still requires handfeeding. Although some breeders and pet stores will sell such birds at a cheaper price, I strongly recommend against it. Handfeeding requires a great deal of skill and experience, and any mistake can result in the chick's death. Even long-time professional breeders occasionally lose a baby to error, miscalculation, or minor problems that suddenly snowball into major problems. Unweaned chicks are also highly susceptible to infection and disease, because their immune systems are not yet fully mature.

One argument that I hear frequently when someone is trying to justify the sale of young chicks is that handfeeding

closely with their housemates. There is nothing sadder than a bird that is purchased on a whim, then given away or returned when the family tires of its new amusement. Some of these birds go from home to home, as they are passed from one inexperienced owner to the next. (I call these "bouncers.") These parrots soon learn to distrust humans and will eventually develop antisocial behaviors because they're being denied the opportunity to bond naturally. It takes a great deal of love and patience to win the trust of one of these bouncers.

by the new owner is necessary so that the chick will bond properly to the owner. This is utter nonsense. Parrots are intelligent, sensitive creatures, and they will bond easily at any age, provided they have been properly socialized as youngsters and are being treated with love and respect. If anything, I believe handfeeding by the new owner might set up a scenario for later problems. In the wild, the parents feed a chick and teach it skills until it is able to survive on its own. As soon as the newly independent parrot is able, its instincts tell it to strike out on its own and find a mate. By this time, the parents are about ready to start a new clutch of babies and would be only too happy to unload the adolescent freeloader. At this stage, friction develops between the "teenager" and its parents (sound familiar?). By feeding a chick and establishing yourself in the parent role, I believe you are more likely to encounter rough spots and dominance issues down the road as the bird matures. If a pet store or breeder tries to pressure you into taking an unweaned chick, walk away and find a different source.

FINDING A QUAKER

There are many methods of finding sources for Quakers. Visit a local pet shop you respect and ask the owner or manager if they are able to get baby Quakers. Even if they don't have any in the store, they may be able to find some, and they might be happy to bring the birds in. I frequently get calls from pet shops inquiring about the availability of chicks in my aviary.

You can also contact a breeder directly. To find one, check the classifieds in your local paper or in national bird magazines such as *Bird Talk* or *Bird Times.* If you're aware of any local bird clubs, these are a great source for breeder referrals. Even if you don't find one advertising Quakers, go ahead and call a few anyway. Unlike

Whether you buy from a breeder or a pet shop, take time to observe some birds before making a choice; look for an energetic, healthy, and personable bird.

dog breeders, many bird breeders raise numerous species and can't possibly list them all in a small ad. If they don't have Quakers, they might be able to point you in the direction of a friend who does. Parrot breeding is a relatively small, highly networked world, and breeders tend to route requests and referrals with the efficiency of a switchboard.

Another method of finding a pet Quaker is to visit one of the local bird fairs that crop up in many communities in spring and fall. Bird clubs usually sponsor them, and these events bring together breeders from all over the area to sell birds and supplies. Be very careful, however, if you decide to purchase a pet at one of these events. By bringing all the birds together in one large area, the risk of disease transmission skyrockets. Buy only from a breeder who keeps the cages clean and requires people to use a hand sanitizer before touching the babies. This certainly won't protect the birds from all diseases because most of the really dangerous stuff is airborne, but it will cut down on the ease of transmission. Also, be certain that you know how to contact the breeder after the fair should a problem or questions arise. Although it's uncommon, there have been instances of transient, disreputable brokers unloading unhealthy birds at public shows. Most clubs try to weed out these individuals, but it's not always possible. Be cautious, use common sense, and walk away if you have lingering doubts.

No matter where you purchase your bird, make sure that you feel comfortable with the seller. The birds should look healthy, bright-eyed, and in good feather. Cages should be clean and uncrowded. Keep in mind that parrots, especially babies, do make a terrible mess in a very short time, but the caretaker should at least be making a valiant effort to keep up. Look at what type of food is being offered. If the birds are being fed a seed-only diet, you'll have some work to do

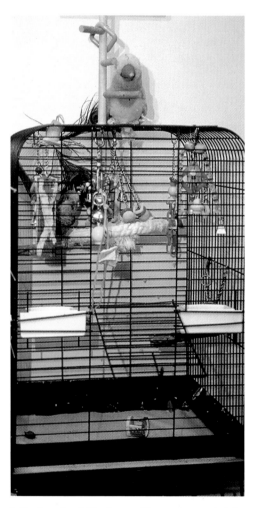

A Quaker should be housed in an appropriately sized cage that is clean and uncrowded; it should also be fitted with suitable perches, toys, and food and water dishes.

Quakers pack a lot of personality into their 11-inch frames. Here, "Elmo" gets acquainted with his two new friends.

converting your new pet to a healthier diet. Fresh fruits, vegetables, and parrot pellets should make up a good portion of what the birds are eating. Watch to see how the seller handles the bird. Though most breeders should be perfectly comfortable handling chicks they've raised, you might see some potential problems. Does the bird appear very nervous or fearful of the person? A few very large or very busy professional breeders are unable (or unwilling) to spend enough time socializing their chicks, so these birds might be shy and slightly wild. On the other hand, be equally cautious of the breeders who

blatantly spoil and refuse to discipline their chicks. Some of these birds mature into little tyrants that will bite or attack any human who dares to displease them. Parrot chicks are adorable, and it's easy to melt when you look into their eyes, but they require behavioral limitations and "rules" like any other youngster. An ideally socialized chick will appear calm, curious, and receptive to displays of affection like head scratching and cuddles. Quakers are very high-energy birds, so a Quaker chick might appear excitable, but shouldn't display any negative emotions such as extreme fear or hostility.

Though not as common as other companion parrots, Quakers are clever and spirited little birds.

A bird needs a calm and quiet transition into a new home, so holidays and special occasions are not the best time to give a bird as a gift.

Of course, even the most perfect bird can have a bad day, so don't write off an otherwise desirable pet because of one minor tantrum. The chick might be tired, stressed, hungry, or overstimulated by activity around it. Come back and visit another day, and see how it acts then. My breeder friends and I have all had the experience of having a perfectly wonderful baby act like an absolute monster at one time or another, usually at a time designed to cause us maximum embarrassment.

HEALTH GUARANTEES

Once you've found an appealing choice, ask the seller about health guarantees. These vary widely, but make certain that it allows you enough time to have the bird examined by a competent avian veterinarian. Understand what your options are if the vet finds a problem. You should be able to return the bird for a full refund if a serious health problem exists or develops within a few days of purchase. Do not expect the seller to pay your veterinary bills. Most health guarantees offer to take the bird back and replace it or refund your money, but I've never known any that will agree to pay for treatments if you decide to keep the bird. Some breeders might be willing to refund a portion of your money if you keep and treat the bird, but this varies widely. One important point to keep in mind: if the unthinkable happens and your new pet dies shortly after you bring it home, refrigerate the body and call the pet shop or breeder *immediately* for further instructions. Many sellers will not accept responsibility for such an expensive pet unless you have a necropsy (animal autopsy) performed by a competent veterinarian. After all, the bird might have died from an accident or even sheer negligence on your part, and the death is in no way the fault of the breeder or shop. In any case, be certain you

When looking for a Quaker, try to find one that you feel an attachment to. You can often tell right away when you've met the right bird for you.

understand how the health guarantee operates, and, if possible, get it in writing.

OTHER CONSIDERATIONS

What about buying a "used" bird, one that has been a previous pet? This can be a great way to find a Quaker if you do a little homework. Why are they getting rid of the bird? Sometimes people are forced to give up beloved pets because of unforeseen life circumstances, and you might be acquiring a gem. Unfortunately, people often dump parrots that have been allowed to develop such nasty habits as biting, screaming, and feather picking. That's not to say that these birds, with a little love and attention, won't blossom into perfect pets, but be aware of the challenges you're facing. In general, if this Quaker is your first parrot and you're relatively inexperienced with birds, you might be better off starting out with one that isn't already carrying a lot of excess emotional baggage. You should also consider how your home environment compares to the bird's former home. For example, if you have five kids, two cats, and a large dog, a Quaker that previously lived with an elderly retired couple might have a difficult time adjusting to your busy household. Quakers are very adaptable

Health guarantees are something to consider when purchasing a new bird—it's always best to have a bird examined by a veterinarian before bringing it home.

Although two Quakers may be able to keep each other company, they are less likely to bond with their human "flockmates" than single birds.

creatures, but it will be easier on both you and the bird if you choose your companion wisely.

Once you find the perfect bird, you may be tempted to buy two so that your new pet has company when you're not home. This is not a good idea! Two Quakers will tend to bond to each other, and will soon consider you an interloper to be chased away. If you want to get a second (or third or fourth...) bird, choose a different species of parrot. If they are of comparable size and temperament, you can allow them to play and interact, but do not allow them to share a cage or they might pair bond even though they are different species. It doesn't matter if the birds are the same sex—they can still bond just as strongly as opposite sex pairs. If you want your pet to stay tame and cuddly, it's important that it considers *you* its mate (or at least its closest platonic friend!).

Housing Your Quaker

Okay, you've searched and questioned and studied, and you've *finally* found the bird of your dreams. Now comes the hard part. Where is it going to live?

Before you bring your new pet home, there's still some work to do. Choosing a suitable cage is every bit as important as choosing the right bird. The wrong cage can

Even though many Quakers will spend a good portion of their time outside a cage, they still need an enclosure for refuge and roosting.

result in a nightmare for both you and your pet. A cage is much more than a simple containment device. To your Quaker, it is a place of physical safety and emotional security. It must be roomy enough to allow sufficient exercise, yet cozy enough to create a sense of well-being. From a human perspective, a cage should be attractive, functional, and easy to maintain, or you will curse it each and every time you're forced to struggle with unwieldy locks, binding trays, or wobbly stands.

THE RIGHT LOCATION

Where you put the cage is another important factor. It's unlikely that either you or your bird will be happy if the cage is placed in a chaotic high traffic location in the house. On the other hand, sticking your new friend in a remote corner where there is little chance to interact with people will almost certainly create a bored and neglected pet. The ideal location is a secure spot in a frequently used room. No, not the bathroom. Kitchens are a bad idea, too, because cooking fumes and cleaning products can cause respiratory distress and even death in birds. Bedrooms aren't a great place to keep a bird either, unless you enjoy being awakened at the first hint of dawn by an exuberant parrot eager to start the day. What this means is that the cage probably should be situated in your living room, dining room, or family room.

CAGE CHOICES

Once you've chosen the spot, you can begin to look at cages. Unfortunately, many

A cage situated in a living area should be attractive and functional, with a mess catcher to prevent spilled food and droppings from soiling the surroundings.

people do it in reverse order: they run out and buy a cage, then spend hours shuffling it about the house in search of a spot it will "fit." Invariably, it doesn't. Make sure you have sufficient room *before* you buy your pet. *Never* subject a bird to a cage that's too small because of limited space. For a Quaker, the minimum cage size is approximately 18 inches x 18 inches x 21 inches. Unless the bird is allowed out for several hours each day, I would recommend an even larger cage. Many common models

Fresh air and sunlight should be available to your bird. Consider placing your bird's cage or play area near a window to catch the early morning sun.

Quakers can certainly be at home within a collection of other species, but you should exercise caution with larger parrots such as Amazons.

of parrot cages are available in 20-inch square by 25-30 inches high, and would offer an active Quaker a little more room to play and romp.

I've been asked if there is such a thing as a cage that's *too* big. Although some other experts might disagree, I think that putting a pet parrot in an extremely large cage can indeed be detrimental. Remember, you are not trying to duplicate the bird's entire original habitat—obviously, no cage can do that. You are trying instead to duplicate the bird's roosting/nesting area. In other words, the place where your bird can go to feel secure from predators and rivals—his "turf." Quakers are extremely territorial birds and too large of an enclosure may make your pet feel insecure. After all, that's quite a lot of territory to defend. If you do

go with a very large cage (more than 36 inches square) make sure that your Quaker has some safety spots, such as a high partially covered perch or a nesting box to sleep in. I have seen birds in large cages sleep huddled amongst their toys for security. Even very tame and trusting pets hate to sleep out in the open. Many bird suppliers now offer items like open roosting boxes, birdie sleeping tents, and other products designed to foster a sense of security.

After you've decided on the size of the cage, the next point to consider is bar spacing. The bars must be close enough together so that the bird can't stick its head out and get hurt, but if they are too close together your little destructor will grab the bars and crimp them together. In most cases, the manufacturer will space the bars

Quakers love to climb, whether on playstands or on the vertical and horizontal bars of a cage.

likely to get soiled. Vertical bars usually look more attractive and show off the bird better. Many manufacturers will compromise by running the front and back bars vertically, and the side bars horizontally. Unless your Quaker is handicapped and has difficulty climbing, bar direction is not really that important—most birds soon become adept at scaling vertical bars, and most owners become adept at scraping poop off the horizontal ones. Ease of cleaning, however, is something you should consider carefully. Some cages are designed with lots of little nooks and crannies that attract debris and fight your best efforts to clean them. Ideally, find someone who is using a cage like the one you want to purchase and ask them about it, or better yet, take a look at the cage in use. Be alert to potential problem areas. If cleaning that particular cage is a major headache, you'll soon regret your purchase.

appropriately for the bird, but you need to be clear about what size of bird the manufacturer intends the design to be used for. In other words, cage size alone is not an indicator of what species can safely use the cage—there are very large flight style cages with thin narrow barring designed for finches and canaries, and very small yet widely barred cages that are used as temporary or travel cages for larger parrots. There also are a fair number of cages on the market that are just badly designed and shouldn't be used at all. In general, bar spacing of half-inch to three-quarter inch is suitable for Quakers.

Your next consideration is bar direction. Bars that run horizontally are easier for the bird to climb, yet more

What about buying a used cage? Though this can be a money-saving temptation, you must proceed cautiously. First, think about why the previous occupant vacated. If the bird that lived in the cage died of an infectious disease, there's a good possibility that the cage may harbor dangerous organisms. Many viruses live for an extraordinarily long time on surfaces and can be passed on to the next victim through contact. If you purchase such a cage, scrub and disinfect *thoroughly*. I can't emphasize this enough—a half-hearted cleaning with dish soap will not kill viruses, and your bird will be at serious risk.

Next, take a careful look at the condition of the cage. Peeling paint, worn plating, or loose welds all can pose a safety hazard. If the cage requires replacement parts, make sure you can identify the manufacturer and check on the availability of parts. Many cages being sold in the United States today are imports, and frequently no replacement parts are available. Even if you can replace parts, ask about cost before you grab your "bargain." In some cases, a broken bottom tray can cost nearly half the price of a whole new cage.

Whether you buy new or used, take a close look at the cage with an eye for safety. Sharp edges, gaps that can catch toes, and heavy guillotine-style doors are all accidents waiting to happen. I have a theory that most active parrots spend a large portion of their day dreaming up ways to hurt themselves (especially on holiday weekends when no vet can be found), so I do my best to anticipate and disarm. You'll also need to make sure that the cage and stand are sturdy enough that they won't get knocked over. I have two very large and very clumsy dogs that accidentally sent more than one cage crashing to the floor before I caught on.

While most standard parrot cages are plated wire or powder-coated wrought iron, there are a few designs popping up in other materials. Never use a cage for your Quaker that is wood, bamboo, or fine wire. Quakers are busy chewers with strong beaks, and they will demolish such a cage promptly. Make sure that the cage is actually intended for a live bird. Some fancy imported metal cages are showing up on the market that are intended for decorative use only. These cages may contain lead or toxic coatings that can kill your pet. Deal only with reputable pet cage manufacturing companies.

Some of the newer materials in cage design are acrylic and stainless steel. Stainless steel is beautiful and trouble free, but very expensive. If you can afford it, this could be a great choice. Acrylic cages are easy to clean and showcase the bird nicely, but I'm not entirely convinced that they're the proper choice for climbing birds like parrots. Some acrylic manufacturers use a combination of acrylic and wire, or place

A cage should include an assortment of toys, perches, and swings; wood accessories are good for chewing, but are more difficult to disinfect.

Be aware of hidden dangers such as ceiling fans that may threaten your Quaker when it is allowed to spend time outside of its cage.

cutouts in the panel so that the bird can still climb. One additional point to consider on acrylic: this is a relatively soft surface that can scratch or dull after time. Ask about availability and cost of replacement panels, or you may find yourself replacing the cage rather than view your pet through a cloudy haze.

ACCESSORIZE

Just like any new home, buying it is only the first step. Now comes the fun part: furniture! Although your Quaker won't require a recliner and big-screen TV, its cage furnishings are just as important to its welfare. Begin with the perches. The cage will usually come with a plain wooden dowel perch or two. One main perch of this sort is fine, but you'll need a few more styles for variety. Adult parrots usually don't lie down (unless they're playing or sick) so they will be standing on their feet 24 hours a day for life. A bird that has just one plain smooth perch will often develop sores on its feet or hocks. Your Quaker needs a variety of sizes, textures, and shapes to properly exercise its feet and prevent these pressure sores. I recommend at least two different perches in addition to the standard dowel—one natural branch perch (manzanita is a great choice) and one cement or terra cotta "pedicure perch." Manzanita perches are readily available in a variety of diameters and can be purchased to bolt onto the side of the cage. Other hardwoods such as ribbon wood, cactus, driftwood, and grapevine sometimes show up in pet stores and catalogs and will work just fine.

Cement pedicure perches come in a variety of sizes, colors, and textures. These are great for trimming your pet's nails and beak if the bird actually uses them. I like to position one of these in a high corner of the cage. My birds then use them as "sleepy perches," so they are on them a minimum of eight hours or so a day. The birds seem to find the rough texture pleasant for sleeping on, probably because there's less danger of slipping off during a restless night. Some people have questioned whether the harsh texture can cause foot sores or abrasions, but I've never found that to happen, at least not in the larger birds. On the contrary, these perches seem to "toughen" the feet slightly. I doubt the birds would use them if they were the least bit uncomfortable, but

Perches should be of varying sizes to provide your bird's feet with exercise and to avoid potential foot problems such as sore spots.

in my experience birds love them. They'll also work to keep the beak in trim if your pet uses them to wipe its beak after eating.

Other commonly sold perches are PVC pipe and rope. PVC is inexpensive, easy to clean, and nearly indestructible. If you choose this, however, make sure to roughen the surface with sandpaper and a file or your Quaker will find them too slippery. Rope perches are fun and provide a soft perching surface, but there are a few inherent dangers. They are difficult to clean and disinfect, so replace them when they get grungy. Birds that chew and fray the rope and birds with overgrown toenails run the risk of getting

Regular bathing is a fun activity that is greatly anticipated by most Quakers; it also helps keep a bird's plumage shiny and healthy.

A shallow crock or dish can serve as a bathtub for a Quaker; the best "tub" will be heavy enough to prevent a bird from tipping it over.

entangled. Again, keep a close watch and replace as necessary.

Once the cage is properly situated and outfitted with a variety of perches, you should next consider food dishes. Although the cage probably comes with a set, you might want to change styles or add extras for treats. The best dishes are stainless steel, heavy unbreakable plastic, or ceramic crocks. Avoid galvanized or painted dishes. These are probably imports and could contain lead, zinc, or other toxins. If your cage came with these types, replace them. Dishes should be large enough to hold an adequate supply of food and water, but not so large that they become a playground. I've seen Quakers that treat large food and water crocks as swimming pools and sandboxes. Slightly smaller dishes will discourage these games. Once you've found a style both you and your bird can live with, immediately buy a duplicate (maybe even triplicate) set. You'll always have a clean set of dishes and won't be tempted to skimp on cleaning. I toss one set in the dishwasher while the clean set goes in the cage. Before, it was easy to give a cursory rinse to the dirty bowls when I was in a hurry. This is like playing Russian roulette with bacteria. Quakers especially like to foul their water with food pieces, toys, and droppings, creating a dangerous bacterial soup. Proper disinfection will keep your bird healthy in spite of itself.

CLEANLINESS IS KEY

Daily disinfection of the food and water bowls is only one part of safe birdie housekeeping. Regular cage cleaning is a must. I don't recommend using litter on the cage bottoms. Corncob, pine shavings, and crushed walnut all give the cage a nice appearance, but I believe they add greatly to the cost and time of upkeep. If not changed frequently, these litters can harbor nearly lethal levels of mold and bacteria. Changing them daily is expensive and a lot of work, and because they don't *look* that bad most people will get a little lazy and let it go a week or so. Again, this is a dangerous practice that could harm your bird. Besides, many birds toss the stuff all over and make a real mess on surrounding carpeting and floors. I now use plain white lightly waxed paper on the cage floors. I buy it special order through a paper company to fit my cages, but rolls of freezer paper (the kind your butcher wraps meat in) work just as well. Actually, any plain paper will work. Newspaper is fine, but I avoid it because I also own white cockatoos. When I used newspaper, my white cockatoos were gray because they always managed to smear the ink on their feathers (it's a cockatoo thing). Yes, some Quakers will immediately run to the bottom of the cage and gleefully rip the paper to shreds. If yours do this, try moving

Natural branches, provided they are not poisonous or treated with chemicals, can serve as perches in a cage or can be mounted as a playstand.

Thorough cleaning and disinfecting is essential to prevent the spread of harmful bacteria and disease. A variety of products can help make the task easier.

the bottom grill up if your cage will allow. If not, keep changing it and try to distract them. Even if they do tear it up, it's still easier to clean up than strewn pine shavings. One friend of mine, after months of exasperation, had a thin sheet of acrylic cut to fit the bottom of the cage. She simply sweeps off the debris and wipes it down each day. Since these acrylic sheets are used as replacement windows in screen doors, any hardware store should have them in stock and be able to cut it for you if you choose this route.

Depending on the number of birds you own and their degree of messiness, you'll want to schedule periodic heavy-duty cleaning. This may be as often as once a week or as infrequent as a few times a year. You will definitely want to do this if any of your birds have been sick or have been exposed to sick or unfamiliar birds. First,

remove your pet from its cage and confine it to a safe place. Next, remove everything from the cage— toys, perches, dishes, etc. I usually toss these items in the sink for a thorough scrubbing and a run through the dishwasher wherever possible. Items that are too big to fit the dishwasher are divided into two piles: porous and non-porous. Non-porous items can be soaked in disinfectant and carefully rinsed. Porous items have to be evaluated one at a time. Wooden toys are a good example. If I'm doing a routine cleaning and not dealing with a disease outbreak, I scrub them up and let them dry thoroughly. If a bird has been sick, I'll usually just discard the toy. It's less expensive to buy a new toy than it is to replace a beloved pet. Once all items have been removed, scrub the cage carefully and rinse well. Once you've finished this step, you're ready to disinfect.

There is a vast array of disinfectants on the market, and it can get pretty confusing. What you really need to understand, however, is that *disinfectants are not cleaners, and vice versa.* Yes, there are some products that call themselves multi-purpose disinfectants and cleaners. Another whole book could be written on this topic, but currently there are no products on the market that can safely and effectively do both. True disinfection is a four-step process: you must first thoroughly clean the item, then rinse it, then apply disinfectant, then rinse again. Disinfectants also have what is known as a "contact time." This is the minimum amount of time that the item must spend in contact with the chemical for it to do its job. In most cases, this time is about ten minutes. You also must keep in mind that the object needs to remain wet with disinfectant during this whole period. If you spray the cage lightly and the product evaporates after four or five minutes, it will not have had a chance to kill all the disease-causing organisms. For small items, it's best to immerse them in a bucket of solution for the recommended contact time. Large items like cages should be wiped or sprayed repeatedly to keep them wet. Some popular brand names include Wavicide-01, Oxyfresh Dent-A-Gene, Virkon-S, Vanodine, and Nolvasan. You can purchase most of these through your veterinarian or through mail-order catalogs. Once you've disinfected, rinse and dry everything thoroughly. This also is a good time to check for damaged, frayed, or cracked items that could pose a safety hazard. You're now ready to put your pet back in its clean safe home!

ON THE ROAD

Finally, there is one more part of the cage issue to explore: travel cages. Even if you don't plan on bringing your Quaker with you on vacation, you still will need some sort of transport cage for trips to the vet or groomer. A cardboard box is not suitable! Your parrot can quickly chew its way to freedom and escape. A box does not allow the bird anything to grip, and your pet will be tossed about and frightened. For a small investment, you can purchase something that will be safe and easy to handle.

There are a few options. Some people simply buy a very small cage to use for transport only. This will certainly work, but may still be awkward to carry and

Many common household plants are poisonous, so never let your bird chew on them.

store. Some manufacturers make collapsible suitcase-style cages that have carrying handles and fold up when not in use. Clear acrylic carrying boxes are available in a variety of sizes and shapes, and they are easy to clean and disinfect when used to transport sick birds to and from the vet. My personal favorites are plastic "pet taxis" commonly used to transport dogs and cats. These are easy to clean, durable, and usually come apart for storage and cleaning. Most of these have a front grill that the bird can hold to prevent sliding. It's an easy matter to drill a small hole on either side to connect a perch across if your bird is going to be in the carrier for longer periods, such as shipping. In fact, these are commonly used as shipping crates for animals, and most are airline approved. I also like the fact that these carriers are solid plastic, making them dark and cozy for the bird. On the few occasions I've used see-through acrylic carriers, my pets have been more nervous. Whatever you choose, this is an important item to own. Even if you never plan on taking your Quaker from the house, a transport cage is vital to have in case of emergency. You may not use it often, but I can guarantee you'll be glad to have it when the need arises.

Nutrition for a Healthy Quaker

One of the fastest ways to shorten your Quaker's life is to feed it an inadequate diet. Unfortunately, that's exactly what many well-meaning pet owners do. A quick walk through the bird department of almost any pet store shows bag after bag of seed mixes, marked with terms like "parrot diet" or "for small hookbills." It would be easy to assume that these mixes are a complete and balanced diet for your pet.

Actually, nothing could be further from the truth. A seed-only diet is dangerously high in fat and deficient in most vitamins and minerals. Although a Quaker can live

A nutritious and varied diet provides the basic foundation for a parrot's good health.

on seed alone and even appear to do just fine, such a diet will drastically shorten the bird's potential lifespan and leave it open to a variety of nutritionally related diseases. Birdseed manufacturers are aware of this, and most of the reputable companies offer "fortified" diets or suggest using vitamin supplements along with their products. Seed mixes are fortified in three basic ways. Most commonly, a vitamin-enriched pellet or grain is added to the mix, often brightly colored to attract the bird's attention. Some premium mixes add a wide variety of different ingredients such as dried fruit and vegetables to enhance the nutritional profile. These methods will help only if the bird eats the extra ingredients. If it picks through and chooses its favorite fatty seed (as most birds will) and tosses the rest of the mix on the floor, then you're gaining no benefit from feeding a fortified mix.

The third method of fortification is to coat the seeds with a vitamin mix, usually by spraying extra oil on the seed surface. There are some potential problems with this method as well. First of all, birds crack the seeds and discard the vitamin-coated hull. They have no saliva in their mouths, so it's doubtful that much of the vitamin is actually ingested by the bird. Secondly, the addition of extra oil shortens the shelf life of the product because unrefrigerated oils can go rancid very quickly. Such diets should always be kept in a cool, airtight container or refrigerated once opened.

A SOLID FOUNDATION

What then *should* you feed your pet? The key is to provide a solid foundation of nutrition, and offer plenty of fresh foods for variety. The easiest way to achieve this is to begin with one of the many excellent formulated (or "complete") diets now on the market. There are two types of these available: pelleted and extruded. Pelleted diets take a mixture of ground ingredients and press them into small, usually tubular pieces (think of guinea pig food). Extruded diets also begin with a mixture of ground ingredients, which is cooked to enhance digestibility and then forced through a die and shaped in a process called extrusion (think of dry cat or dog food). Pellets usually have a coarser grain and are plainer looking, while extruded diets have a finer texture and are available in a wide array of shapes, colors, and sizes. To confuse the matter slightly, most people (and many books) in the pet bird industry refer to all formulated diets as "pellets," even though the majority of available diets today are actually extruded. At any rate, either of these products can serve as a base diet for your Quaker.

When choosing which brand to feed your bird, look for a product that is well known and easily available. Most of the larger manufacturers have dedicated years of research into the development of their products, and they strive to incorporate new information as it becomes available. In the past, all ideas about parrot nutrition were based on what constituted a healthy diet for chickens. It wasn't until about the

1980s that researchers began to take a closer look at nutritional deficiencies in pet birds and finally realized that parrots aren't poultry. For example, chickens do not need vitamin C—they manufacture it in their digestive tracts. For that reason, pet bird products usually did not contain vitamin C. We now know that at least some parrots (lories, hanging parrots, fig parrots, and perhaps others) do indeed need a dietary source of vitamin C, and most manufactured diets and supplements now contain it.

Once you've identified a few brands that are readily available in your area, you can pick one based on a recommendation from your veterinarian, pet store, or bird breeder, or you can buy small quantities of a few different types and let your bird choose its favorite. Although many experts say that you should pick one brand and stick to it, I disagree. I regularly rotate between about five or six well-respected brands, depending on price, availability, and whim. One of the most frequent arguments against formulated diets is that the birds get bored eating the same thing every day. Although I'm not sure I agree entirely with this view (most birds are creatures of habit and seem to find security in sameness), I don't want my birds to become fixated on any particular

Although pelleted diets are designed to be "complete," most experts recommend that a Quaker's diet also include some seeds, nuts, as well as fruits and vegetables.

Treats such as seed cakes and millet spray should not form the bulk of a parrot's diet. They are especially useful for training and positive reinforcement.

food. Quakers are sometimes a little rigid in their habits, and feeding them the same diet for months on end might cause them to refuse other foods. By feeding a variety of brands, you will know that your pet is getting excellent basic nutrition, and it should never become bored or stuck in a rut.

GET FRESH

Although formulated diets are often referred to as "complete" diets, I believe that parrots also need a variety of fresh foods and treats for stimulation and enjoyment. I feed my birds a ratio of 70 to 80 percent extruded diet, and 20 to 30 percent fruits, vegetables, seeds, nuts, and "people food." (Most Quakers would *kill* for a piece of pizza). Avoid salty or sugary treats, and *never* give your pet avocado or chocolate—both are highly toxic to birds. I like to give my birds nutritionally dense fruits and vegetables like kale, sweet potatoes, broccoli, carrots, kiwi, cantaloupe, and berries. It is important to remember that certain fruits and vegetables will temporarily change the color and consistency of the bird's droppings. Juicy

Fresh fruit and vegetables can be offered daily. All should be chemical-free and chopped for easy consumption, then removed after several hours to prevent spoilage.

items can cause runny, highly liquid droppings. Beets, pomegranates, and most berries will stain droppings deep red or purple. This is perfectly normal and not a cause for concern. (Of course, if your pet ever shows changes like this and *has not been* eating fresh foods, or if he appears fluffed up and lethargic, it could be a sign of illness. If you're unsure, call your veterinarian.)

Other favorites include grapes, bananas, red or green peppers, and fresh peas. All my pets love apples and corn on the cob, and although these aren't loaded with as many vitamins as some of the other choices, they still make a great treat. Some birds also love meat, especially chicken. Just be certain it's properly cooked and cooled first. In general, if it's good (healthy) for humans, it's probably good for your bird.

If you're so inclined, you can even cook for your Quaker. Several manufacturers now offer cooking mixes that include ingredients such as rice, beans, and pasta. You can make large batches of these and freeze the unused portions for later use. I stick the cooked mixture in an ice cube tray, and then place the tray in a large freezer bag. When I want to give my pets a treat, I pop out a few cubes and defrost them in the microwave (be very careful to check for hot spots before offering to your bird). Or, concoct your own recipes using a variety of beans, rice, and other grains. My birds love really spicy stuff, so I toss in lots of garlic or chili powder, and it's always a big hit. One caution: when feeding any soft (perishable) food, always remove it from the cage after about four hours. These foods spoil rapidly and become a breeding ground for harmful

A finicky Quaker may need encouragement to try a new food. Be patient—it can take days and even weeks for the big moment to occur.

THE GUIDE TO OWNING A QUAKER PARROT

It is especially important to limit the amount of treats you provide, because Quakers, like other parrots, can quickly develop favorite foods.

bacteria, which can make your bird very sick.

To round out the diet, offer your Quaker small amounts of seeds and nuts. Millet seed sprays are a common treat, and your pet will enjoy working its way through one of these. A good quality seed mix designed for small parrots makes a great snack, but limit the quantity and frequency so that you don't create a "seed junkie." Seeds are to birds sort of like what potato chips are to people, so it's easy for them to overindulge and ignore healthier food choices. Some Quakers relish nuts, especially walnuts, pecans, and almonds. Of course you'll have to crack the shells first, but your bird will have fun digging out the nutmeats.

SUPPLEMENTS AND OTHER EXTRAS

What about all the supplements on the market? If your bird is eating a diet pretty much like the one described above, then supplements shouldn't be necessary. Be honest, though. If you put healthy foods in the dish each morning, but your Quaker tosses them out and so you feel guilty and fill the dish with seed each evening, then your bird isn't really eating a balanced diet. Healthy food is only healthy if your bird actually *eats* it. If you own a picky eater, you must gradually, yet firmly, convince the bird to accept the diet you've chosen. Over time, even the most determined "seed-aholics" will begin to accept new foods once they know you're serious and aren't going to cave in every time they toss the food or sulk. As I said before, birds are creatures of habit. Once the rejected food becomes a familiar item in their dish, they'll gradually decide that it's edible and that you're not attempting to poison them. Most picky birds are owned by people who offer a new food item once or twice, then give up because "my bird won't eat that." I once spoke with a woman whose pet Quaker refused to eat anything but a basic seed mix. I urged her to choose one healthy food and offer it to her bird every day for a solid month and see what happened. For 28 days she dutifully chopped up carrots and placed them on top of the seed, and for 28 days the Quaker dutifully screeched, pitched the carrots onto the floor, and glared at her angrily. To her amazement, on day 29 the bird stared thoughtfully at the carrots for a long moment, then reached down and took a bite. By the next morning, he had decided that carrots were his favorite food, and now becomes visibly upset if they aren't in his bowl!

Although not all Quakers are quite this stubborn, you should not decide what your bird likes or dislikes based on just a few attempts. Like children, they need to experience different foods and acquire a taste for certain healthy items. Once your pet is eating a wide variety of foods and is willing to experiment with unfamiliar fare,

then you can plan a diet that takes its favorites into consideration.

If your bird is not yet eating a balanced diet, or if it has been ill or under stress, then vitamin supplements might be in order. Most bird vitamins come in either a liquid form that can be added to the drinking water, or a powdered form that can go in the water or be sprinkled over soft foods. I prefer the powders because I believe they're more stable. Whenever possible, add the supplements to soft food, not the water. Drinking water quickly becomes contaminated as the bird drinks, bathes, plays, and dunks food. Adding vitamins, which often use dextrose (sugar) as a base, helps create a "bacterial soup." If you do decide to add them to the water, then I recommend you change it twice a day. Either way, make sure your bird has clean, fresh water at all times.

In addition to vitamins, there are other supplements marketed for pet birds. Some of these are helpful, some unnecessary, and a few might be downright dangerous. Grit and charcoal should *never* be used for parrots. In the past, both of these products were sold as digestive aids for birds. Though small amounts of grit may be useful to certain species, such as pigeons or canaries, parrots do not require grit and can become dangerously ill if they consume too much. Charcoal used to be touted as a blood purifier, among other things. In fact, it inhibits the absorption of vitamins and minerals and can cause serious deficiencies.

On the other hand, there are a few digestive aids on the market that might enhance your bird's health. "Probiotics" are mixtures of several species of beneficial bacteria that normally populate the digestive tract and keep bad bacteria and yeast fungus out. Yogurt usually contains probiotics—if you take a look at most brands, they will say "contains active cultures" or something along those lines. Although you can give your pet yogurt, bird-specific products exist (usually in powdered form) that you simply sprinkle over food. Probiotics can be given at any time, but they are especially useful if your bird is stressed or on antibiotics, which upset the natural flora of the digestive tract. Of course, always check with your veterinarian before giving any supplements to a sick bird.

Other supplements, such as digestive enzymes, herbal formulas, and homeopathic remedies may or may not be helpful. Most of these will cause no harm to your pet (assuming they are recommended for use in birds), but there's a wide range of these products, and though some are excellent, others are useless. Unless you're operating on a recommendation from your vet or a trusted bird expert, proceed cautiously and don't be afraid to call the manufacturer and ask questions about their research and quality control. Above all, don't attempt to use *any* product as a substitute for proper veterinary care. Supplements should be used to prevent deficiencies and to enhance the vitality of an already healthy bird, not to "cure" a sick bird that hasn't been properly diagnosed.

Table foods can make up a small portion of your Quaker's diet, as long as they are nutritious dishes such as oatmeal or pasta.

Health Care

Although Quakers are generally pretty hardy birds, you must remember that if an accident or illness does strike, your pet is completely dependent upon you to take the proper course of action. Any delay or inattention could cost your bird its life. For this reason, a little advance planning makes a lot of sense.

FIND A BIRD DOCTOR

The first thing you must do is choose an avian veterinarian. Bird care is totally different from dog or cat care, and even the best dog clinic in town might be unable to provide adequate treatment for a feathered client. Ask for recommendations from your bird's breeder or local bird shops, or contact the Association of Avian Veterinarians (see Resources) for the name of a qualified practitioner in your area.

Of course, if you live in a remote rural area, you might find that the nearest bird-friendly animal clinic is hours away. If this is the case, your best bet is to find a local veterinarian that you trust, and then discuss the situation. Ask him or her how they would proceed if your bird were injured or ill. Some will not see birds at all. Others will accept birds as patients, then work closely by telephone with a more avian-experienced colleague. Be certain that you are both comfortable with the plan. The absolute worst-case scenario is to be thumbing randomly through a phone book seeking a veterinarian when your pet is lying bleeding or desperately ill on the cage floor. Please plan ahead, and do not put yourself (or your bird) in this position.

Once you've found a vet that you like, the next step is to decide on an exam schedule. I always bring a new bird in for a health check, both for the bird's welfare and for my own. Although it's uncommon, there are a few bird diseases that can transmit to humans. Most of these don't present much danger to healthy adults, but if you have elderly or immune-compromised individuals in your household then you definitely should not bring a bird (or any other animal) into your home until it receives a clean bill of health.

Your Quaker's first health check should start with a thorough physical exam. To begin, the bird should be weighed, and its weight compared to normal ranges for other healthy Quakers. Often a subtle weight loss is the first indication of illness. Once you know what is normal for your pet, this will be a valuable indicator of its health in future exams. The doctor then will look at its eyes, ears, nostrils, and mouth for any sign of inflammation or discharge. Unlike dogs and cats, birds are not usually monitored for temperature, but the doctor should use a stethoscope to listen to the heart, and check for any signs of breathing difficulty or abnormality. Some vets palpate the bird's body to detect any unusual swellings or possible tumors, and gently tug on or bend its legs and wings to check for stiffness, lameness, or signs of discomfort. If your Quaker will oblige, a sample dropping can be collected to look for intestinal parasites. Several other tests, including gram stains and cultures to detect bacterial infections, complete

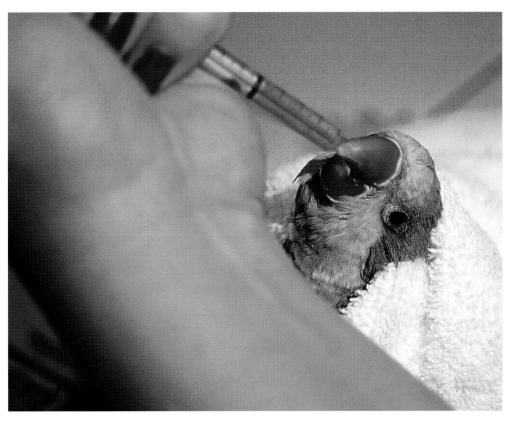

An avian veterinarian may in some cases prescribe a course of medication, which may be administered orally with a syringe.

blood counts and chemistry panels to gauge overall health, as well as screening for various diseases are available and might be recommended. Some clinics offer package prices for running several tests at once, and this usually will save you some money. This is also a great time to have grooming tasks done, such as wing and nail clips or beak trimming.

What about vaccinations? Although there are a few vaccines on the market that prevent a host of deadly viruses, in most cases these aren't necessary for single pets. If you already have other birds at home, tell your veterinarian what species you own and discuss any previous

A yearly exam by a veterinarian may detect unseen health complications; such exams are especially important for households with multiple birds.

health problems or unexplained deaths among your pets. Sometimes a seemingly healthy animal can be a carrier for disease and will infect others without ever becoming sick itself. In a case like this, vaccinations might be in order. Also, if you plan on bringing your Quaker to bird shows or club meetings where it will be around other birds, then you run a much higher risk of exposing it to disease. These are all issues you need to discuss with your veterinarian so that you can decide on the proper course of action to best protect your pet.

SIGNS OF ILLNESS

Although the best approach for any disease is prevention, sometimes illness happens in spite of our precautions. In this case, early detection and prompt treatment can spell the difference between life and death. Unfortunately, birds are experts at hiding signs of sickness until they're seriously ill. In the wild, a sick or weak bird would be targeted as an easy dinner by predators, so every instinct tells it to act healthy and try to keep up with the flock for as long as possible. By knowing what's normal behavior for your pet, you'll be able to recognize early symptoms of illness and act promptly.

A sick bird might act lethargic, lose interest in eating or playing, or become less vocal. It will probably fluff up its feathers to maintain body heat, and might sit slumped down on its perch. It's important to distinguish between "sick bird posture" and "sleepy bird posture."

Weight loss can be a symptom of illness in birds, so it's a good idea to use a scale to monitor your bird's weight on a regular basis.

A healthy but sleepy bird will yawn, fluff up, and squat down on the perch on one leg while it folds the other leg up against its belly. Its eyes might be half-closed, yet it is still alert and will spring to attention if something startles or interests it. A sick bird will fluff up, squat low on the perch on both legs, and it might have trouble keeping its eyes open. Sometimes the eyes look glassy or unfocused. The bird also might have trouble breathing—if you hear any clicking or wheezing sounds, or see its tail bob up and down as it takes a breath, then it's probably having respiratory problems. A change in the color, consistency, or frequency of the droppings can also signal illness. Normal bird droppings consist of three parts: the feces, which should be well formed and are usually green or brown in color; urine,

which should be clear; and urates, which should be white. Runny, unformed feces, or urates that are tinted green or yellow might indicate a problem, especially when combined with other symptoms. A seriously ill bird will be too weak to perch and will crouch down on the cage floor. A bird in this condition is probably near death and needs help right away.

If your pet ever exhibits any of these signs, *call your veterinarian immediately.* Don't attempt to use one of the over-the-counter medications often sold in pet stores. Most of these are useless for birds, and some can actually cause more harm. The most helpful thing you can do is to keep the bird warm until you can reach a vet. A sick Quaker loses body heat very quickly, and an external heat source can be a lifesaver. If it's in the early stages (only showing minor signs of

Careful observation of your bird is one of the best ways to detect subtle signs of illness such as labored breathing, fluffed feathers, and lack of appetite.

illness), and your pet is still active, then covering the cage and placing a heating pad on top might generate enough extra warmth. If the bird is noticeably weak or is on the cage floor, you need to warm it as quickly as possible. The easiest way to do this is to place the bird on a soft towel in a small cardboard box or pet carrier, with a heating pad or hot water bottle under the towel. Position the heat source so that it covers only half the box, so that the bird can move away if it gets too hot. Make sure there's sufficient airflow and monitor it frequently to avoid overheating (a too-warm bird will pant and hold its wings away from its body). Some sporting goods stores sell inexpensive air-activated disposable heating pads that are perfect for emergencies like this. Please remember that putting a sick bird on heat is critical, but it is only a temporary supportive measure until you can get to the veterinarian's office. Without further treatment, it's not likely to recover.

Once you arrive at the vet's office, the doctor will recommend the appropriate tests. The most common bird diseases are bacterial or viral, although parasitic problems show up occasionally. Sometimes two different problems exist at the same time, making diagnosis and treatment a little more difficult. For example, nutritional deficiencies from a poor diet can weaken the immune system so that the bird frequently contracts bacterial infections. Although antibiotics might clear it up, unless the underlying problem (the poor diet) is corrected, the infections will recur.

In fact, bacteria rarely overwhelm a healthy, strong bird (or human). We're constantly bombarded by all kinds of nasty germs in our environment, and most of the time our immune systems keep the intruders at bay. It's usually when we're stressed, run down, or facing other physical challenges that things start to break down and we become ill. For example, a few years ago my town was doing some work on the water supply mains during an unusually hot summer.

Within days, two of my birds became violently ill. My mother-in-law (who lives with us) also complained of stomach cramps and nausea. My husband and I, and the rest of our flock (more than 50 parrots), were fine. It turned out to be an outbreak of *E. coli* bacteria, probably from the water. Interestingly, both the sick birds and my mother-in-law are older and had some other minor health problems to begin with. The rest of us were able to fight it off and stay healthy. Of course, many types of bacteria are deadly, so it's always important to avoid contamination. My point is that feeding your bird a healthy diet and making it feel safe and happy will go a long way toward building a strong immune system and helping it resist infection.

Besides bacterial infections, there are many other diseases that can endanger your Quaker. Psittacosis (also known as Ornithosis, Chlamydiosis, and Parrot Fever) is a relatively common problem in pet birds, although improved testing and treatment options have greatly reduced its occurrence. Psittacosis is caused by *Chlamydia psittaci,* which is an odd pathogen that shares features with both bacteria and viruses. It is curable with certain antibiotics, although the treatment is lengthy (45-60 days).

Fresh air and sunlight are good for your Quaker's health, but a bird should never be allowed to become overheated or chilled.

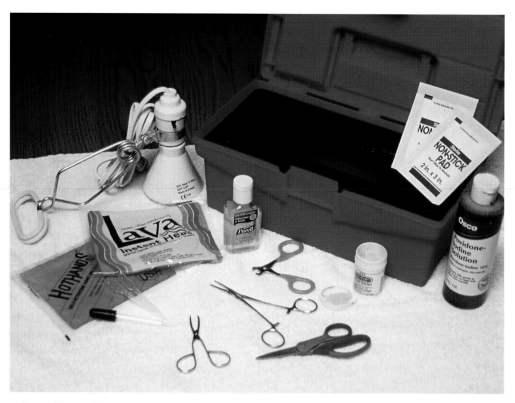

A first aid kit could save your Quaker's life in an emergency; always have one on-hand, both at home and when traveling.

Because this disease is highly contagious to other birds, and can infect humans as well, it's important to have any new birds tested. It's usually spread through inhalation of infected particles, such as feather dust or dried feces. Common symptoms include respiratory problems, diarrhea, loss of appetite, and yellow or green urates or urine. Without treatment, birds showing clinical signs of the disease usually will not survive. In humans, Psittacosis often mimics the flu and is rarely fatal. Although it's very unlikely that a healthy adult would contract this disease from a pet Quaker, if you're ever suffering from a flu-like illness that won't go away, you should probably mention to your doctor that you own birds,

especially if your pet has not been tested for *Chlamydia.*

Avian viruses are another serious threat to your Quaker's health, although few if any are transmissible to humans. Though there are dozens of possible viruses that can infect pet parrots, only a few are common. The most common (and most deadly) are Polyomavirus, Pacheco's disease, and Proventricular Dilatation Disease (PDD). These viruses are usually fatal and can spread to other birds in your house. Polyomavirus usually infects unweaned chicks, although it's likely that adult birds can act as carriers of the disease. Symptoms include weight loss, hemorrhaging beneath the skin, feather deformities, and sudden death. There is a vaccine for Polyomavirus, although most veterinarians don't feel it's necessary for single pets. If you have other birds, ask your vet what he or she recommends.

Pacheco's disease is another deadly virus, caused by various strains of *Herpesvirus*. Pacheco's differs in the way it attacks. Some birds become acutely ill, but survive. Others die suddenly, without warning. The virus attacks the liver and spleen, and symptoms can include lethargy, vomiting, green or yellow urates, and diarrhea. There's a vaccine available for Pacheco's, but it's not without side effects, so it usually isn't recommended unless your pet is at high risk from exposure to other birds, especially known carriers.

Probably the worst virus facing parrots today is Proventricular Dilatation Disease (PDD). PDD is always fatal, and to date there is no test or vaccine available. Little is known about the virus and how it transmits, but it attacks the nerves in the digestive tract and causes the bird to slowly starve to death. Accurate diagnosis is difficult in a live bird, but its presence can be confirmed after death by examining tissue samples. Symptoms include weight loss in spite of a good appetite, vomiting, and passing undigested food in the droppings. This is a heartbreaking disease, and not much can be done for infected birds other than supportive care. Much research is being done on PDD, and researchers hope to develop a test and vaccine within the next few years.

ACCIDENTS HAPPEN

Although all these diseases sound pretty scary, if you purchase a healthy Quaker from a reputable breeder or pet store, and keep it clean and well-fed, you're unlikely to encounter most of these problems. In actuality, the biggest threat to your Quaker's health is accidents. Although your house might seem safe and secure to you and your family, the average American household is fraught with danger for an unsupervised parrot. With a little foresight and common

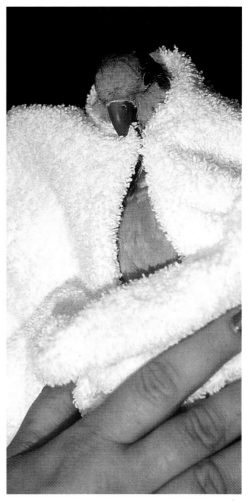

A parrot that is used to being handled in a towel will be less likely to panic when it is being restrained for grooming or medical procedures.

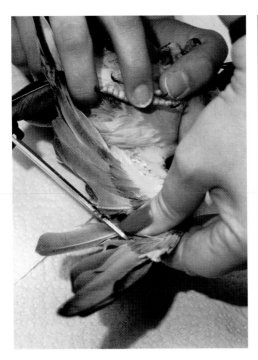

To prevent injury, always point scissors away from a bird when clipping its wings.

help tremendously in restricting their access to trouble.

Even a clipped bird, however, should be supervised carefully when out of the cage. Quakers love to chew, and can't tell the difference between a bird toy and an electrical cord. Don't let your bird walk around on the floor where it might get stepped on or attacked by another pet. Don't let your bird chew on houseplants, which might be poisonous. Even if you know that the plant is non-poisonous, it probably isn't *good* for your pet, and it certainly isn't good for the plant! Parrots are like human toddlers—they can get into trouble in the blink of an eye if you're not watching. If you can't supervise your bird, then put it in the cage where it's safe until you can give it your undivided attention.

If an accident does happen, be prepared. If the bird is unconscious or bleeding, you have to act quickly. For bleeding, you must first find the source of the blood. Often, parrots break feathers that haven't fully emerged from their protective sheaths. These are called "blood feathers," and they can bleed heavily. If there's only a tiny amount of blood (just a few small drops), you can try placing the bird in a quiet, dark place for a few minutes and see if the bleeding subsides. Sometimes these will coagulate on their own, but you will need to keep an eye on the area to make certain it doesn't get re-injured. If the bleeding doesn't stop within a few minutes, or if it begins to bleed more heavily, then you

sense, however, you can prevent most accidents from happening, and be prepared to handle those that do occur.

The single most important thing you can do to protect your bird is to keep its wings properly clipped. Although it might look like fun to have a free-flighted Quaker swooping through your house, this is truly an accident waiting to happen. A crash into a ceiling fan, mirror, or window can instantly kill a bird. Birds are drowned in open toilets, water-filled sinks, and uncovered fish tanks with depressing frequency. (Parrots are lousy swimmers and can't fly up with waterlogged feathers.) In captivity, birds face hundreds of situations that they're not equipped to deal with through instinct and experience, and it's up to us to do our best to protect them. Clipped wings will

THE GUIDE TO OWNING A QUAKER PARROT

will need to pull out the broken feather. Carefully restrain the bird by wrapping it gently in a towel. Hold the wing securely right above the damaged feather. With a pair of needle-nosed pliers, grip the feather close to where it emerges from the skin, and pull it firmly and quickly in the direction it grows. This does hurt, and your pet probably will tell you so in no uncertain terms, but it's the only way to stop the bleeding. If there is bleeding at the wing where the feather was pulled, you can hold gentle pressure on the site with your finger or a gauze pad until it stops. When pulling a blood feather, *always* make sure that you hold the wing right above the damaged feather, thus immobilizing that section. If you hold it too far away, you run the risk of breaking your pet's wing when you yank on the feather.

If the bird is bleeding from a broken toenail or chipped beak, hold a bit of styptic powder (available at most pet stores) against the spot. If you don't have styptic powder on hand, you can use flour or cornstarch, but these won't work quite as well. I suggest you start a birdie first aid kit, so that you have emergency items like gauze, tweezers, styptic powder, and heating pads on hand. If the bleeding is from a skin wound, do not use styptic powder. Hold gentle but firm pressure against the area with a piece of sterile gauze until the bleeding stops. If the wound is tiny and superficial, you can

Being out of its cage can be quite an adventure for a Quaker. It can also expose a curious bird to a whole range of hidden dangers.

Kitchens are filled with hazards for birds—open flames, toxic fumes, cleaning supplies, and dangerous foods. If a bird must be in a kitchen it should be closely watched.

clean it with a solution of chlorhexidine (available from your veterinarian) or an iodine compound, and keep a careful eye out for signs of further infection or complications. If the wound is large or bleeds heavily, hold pressure on it and get the bird to a veterinarian's office or emergency clinic immediately. Even if the bleeding has stopped, the loss of blood and trauma can cause serious complications, and the bird might need sutures, antibiotics, or replacement fluids.

If your Quaker is ever bitten or scratched by a cat, get it to a veterinarian *immediately,* even if the wound is tiny and looks insignificant. Cats carry a bacterium in their saliva that is absolutely deadly to birds, and without proper antibiotics your Quaker could die from even a very minor bite. Even if your bird looks and acts fine, *never* disregard a cat bite.

Burns are another first aid emergency. Curious (and unclipped) parrots can fly onto hot stoves, into cooking pots, or against burning cigarettes. If the burn is superficial, immerse the injured area in cool water if possible and call your veterinarian. Never use human burn ointments on your pet. These are not meant to be ingested, and if your bird preens the area and swallows the ointment it might make the bird sick. Besides, most of these are greasy and will foul the feathers. If the burn is serious, or if the bird appears to be in shock, keep it warm and transport it to a vet or animal emergency clinic immediately.

One of the least obvious but most dangerous threats to your Quaker's life is airborne toxin. Parrots have extremely complicated and delicate respiratory systems. Fumes that might not even irritate you can kill a bird. Remember the legacy of canaries in a coal mine? Old-time miners knew that a bird would die from poisonous gases long before they posed a threat to man. Never spray aerosol products anywhere near your bird, and be equally cautious about cleaners, solvents, paints, varnishes, or any other chemical that might emit fumes. I've also heard stories about birds dying when self-cleaning ovens are turned to a cleaning cycle. If you absolutely must use any of these products, remove your bird to a well-ventilated area in another part of the house, and make certain that fumes aren't being circulated into that room. Many overheated nonstick pans also emit odorless fumes that are lethal to birds. Some non-stick surfaces are safe, but if you're unsure, be

A correctly installed shower perch can provide a Quaker with a safe spot for being misted or bathed.

Take a good look around your home before allowing your bird freedom from its cage. Lead, even from stained glass, is highly poisonous.

very careful to use these pans on low heat only and never let them boil dry. Because I keep birds I use only stainless steel pots and pans in my kitchen.

If this seems like a lot of work and inconvenience to protect your pet, think of it this way: your bird really is a canary in a coal mine, at least as far as your home is concerned. Even if you're willing to risk its life, do you want to breathe (or allow your family to breathe) toxins that are dangerous enough to kill a parrot?

Training Your Quaker

Once your new pet is settled in, it's time to begin training. Training can be as elaborate as teaching your Quaker a wide repertoire of tricks, or as simple as laying down some house rules. The important thing is to develop a mutual respect and understanding between you and your bird so that you know what to expect from each other.

CLIP FIRST, TRAIN LATER

The first thing you must do is clip your bird's wings. You can have the breeder or pet shop do the wing clip before you bring your new pet home, or have your veterinarian do it when you bring the bird in for its first checkup. You can easily learn to perform future clips yourself, but it's best to see one done first. Wing clips cause absolutely no pain to the bird (although your pet might try to convince you otherwise). It's the same as a human having a haircut or getting fingernails cut. The preferred method of clipping is to cut the first eight to ten flight feathers off each wing, right below the overlapping wing covert feathers. With a trim like this, your Quaker can safely glide to the floor if

When done with patience and kindness, training is a wonderful way to bring you and your Quaker closer together.

Properly clipped wings will prevent a bird from flying away but still allow it to glide to the ground without being injured.

frightened, but it will not be able to gain altitude and fly away.

Regular wing trims are essential for your bird's safety, because a fully flighted bird is an accident waiting to happen. It's also difficult if not impossible to properly train a flighted parrot; if it doesn't feel like obeying, it will simply fly away. Finally, due to concerns about escaped Quakers creating feral populations, some states even require by law that pet Quakers be properly and consistently clipped. One word of caution: flight feathers grow back quickly, and a bird with even one or two regrown feathers is capable of flight, especially with a boost from a gust of wind. Check your pet's wings frequently, and trim as needed.

BASIC TRAINING

Once its wings are properly clipped, you can begin basic training. The two most important commands your Quaker must learn are "step up" and "get down." "Step

up" is used to tell a parrot to climb onto an offered hand. This is critical if you wish to pick up your bird or move it from place to place. "Get down" is the reverse command; use this when you want to place your bird on a perch or back in its cage, and you'd like it to release the death grip it has on your finger. Some trainers use the words "step down," but I don't want to risk confusing the bird with two similar "step" commands. You can use any choice of words you want, but make sure you're consistent. Using different words from one session to the next will really confuse your pet.

To teach these commands, begin by placing your Quaker on a training stand or the back of a wooden chair. Press your finger lightly but firmly against the bird's abdomen, at a point right above its legs. Say "step up" while you push gently against the bird. At this point, it has the choice of stepping up or of being pushed over backwards. If the bird steps up onto your finger, praise it lavishly and reverse the procedure: move your finger so that the bird is facing the perch (or chair back) and say "get down." Again, make a big fuss when it obeys. If the bird refuses to step up, and reacts by biting, leaning backwards, or running away, give it a verbal reprimand and gently try again.

I see two common mistakes that people make when attempting to teach this command. The first is placing their finger too high up on the bird's body. If you're pushing against its chest or under its chin, your pet can't get its foot up that high, even if it understands and wants to obey. In this case, the bird will most likely attempt to grab your finger with its beak to maintain its balance, and this action might be misinterpreted by an inexperienced owner as an attempted bite. Make sure you place your finger low enough for the bird to climb up easily.

The second common mistake occurs when the trainer simply places his finger against the parrot's body and repeats "Step up! Come on, be a good bird and step up. Step up now, alright..." Because the trainer isn't actively pushing against it, the bird has no idea what it is supposed to do, and it can't even accurately recognize the command amid the patter of the trainer's voice. Always push against the bird in a firm, fluid movement. The idea is to disturb its balance slightly so that it steps up in an attempt to regain its balance. At the same time, give the command in a clear friendly

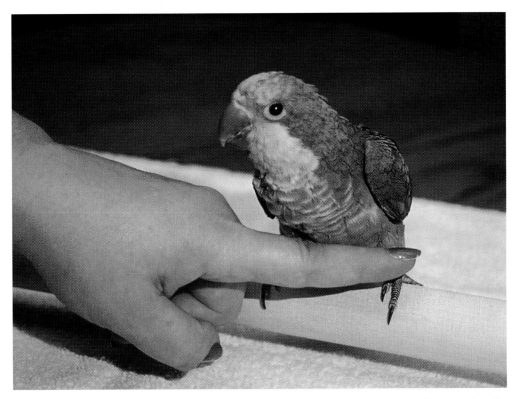

Step up is the first command to teach your Quaker. As you say it, gently press your finger against the bird's abdomen.

A bird must be comfortable being handled before training can begin. Speak softly and move slowly so as to not startle your student.

voice. Do not use additional words or sentences like the example above, or the bird will not know which words to associate with the action. Most parrots learn these two commands easily, as long as you are consistent in using them.

PAY ATTENTION

Next, let's look at what your bird has the right to expect from you. Besides obvious things like fresh food and water and proper veterinary care, your pet has the right to expect attention and affection. As I've stated repeatedly, parrots are sensitive, loving animals that require affection. They aren't solitary creatures like reptiles that do just fine alone. A parrot deprived of any affection and interaction will fail to thrive. If you do not have the ability to spend at least a little one-on-one time with your Quaker every day, then please reconsider your choice of a parrot for a pet.

Your bird also has the right to feel secure and safe in your home. That means adequate caging, protection from predators (dogs, cats, and unruly children), and the knowledge that you will never strike at it or otherwise injure it in a fit of rage. In some households, anger is expressed through screaming, punching, and throwing things. This behavior is just as toxic for birds as it is for other family members. Parrots frequently mirror the dominant emotions in a home. Happy, loving owners usually

Some birds may be reluctant to leave their cage. Such timid birds may be gently coaxed out with food treats.

have happy, loving pets; people who are filled with anger and rage should not be surprised if they end up with a biting, screaming parrot. This is not to imply that you need to dance around the house singing Disney tunes in order to keep your Quaker happy (although it might work). Loving, consistent discipline will quickly teach your bird to act in ways that are acceptable.

DISCIPLINE TACTICS

How do you discipline a bird? Well, that depends a lot on the bird. Some individuals are so sensitive that a harsh glance might be all it takes to stop them in their tracks. A firm "No!" is sufficient in others. Highly active and aggressive birds might need a "time out" where they're returned to their cage, or their cage is covered. Parrots are keenly attuned to human body language, so your Quaker will soon learn when it is getting under your skin.

My pet birds often act up when I'm on the phone or otherwise occupied; they know I can't stop what I'm doing to cover their cage or scold them. At times like this, I often make an exaggerated angry face at them (we call it "giving the hairy eyeball"). Gizmo, my pet Timneh African Grey, will usually turn to the other birds and say

Training a Quaker to talk takes practice, patience, and consistency. Short but frequent sessions are the best way to encourage your bird to speak.

Even a trained bird can get into trouble. To a Quaker, an electrical cord looks like a tempting toy, but it's actually an accident waiting to happen.

"ever' body be quiet! Mommy's mad!" Unfortunately, my cockatoo and my Quaker think this is funny and will continue to be obnoxious. The best punishment for those two is for me to completely ignore them. If a parrot wants attention, it might not really care if you're standing next to its cage talking lovingly or screaming angrily—it only knows that it has your undivided attention. Try giving your bird attention and praise when it's behaving nicely and playing quietly. When it's screaming or otherwise acting up, tell it "no" or "be quiet" in a firm, calm voice, then either leave the room or cover the cage. As soon as it settles down for a few minutes, return to the bird and praise it profusely. It will soon associate good behavior with attention, and unacceptable behavior with

isolation. Never leave a bird covered for punishment for more than ten minutes. If it begins to act up again, you can repeat the procedure, but always come back after a short while and uncover and praise it. The idea is to create a simple cause-and-effect for your bird, not to frustrate and alienate it.

BEHAVIOR ISSUES

You must also be realistic about what constitutes acceptable behavior. Parrots are by nature very vocal creatures, and they seem to be hardwired to greet sunrise and sunset with shrieks and shouts. To punish them for this natural behavior isn't fair. Of course, manic pointless screaming for hours on end is not acceptable, and your bird should learn the difference. In our house, the pets are allowed the morning/evening brief scream fest, occasional shouts of exuberance or irritation during other times, and unlimited jabbering, talking, whistling, and hooting the rest of the day. Extended periods of off-hours, full-lung capacity shrieking will earn them two stern warnings, then punishment. Piper, my Blue-fronted Amazon, acts as room monitor and tells me to "cover the bird" if one of the others is getting out of hand.

Next to screaming, unprovoked biting is another no-no. Again, you need to look at why the bird bites. If it's frightened or hurt, then biting is a natural defense and shouldn't be punished. If it is simply being a brat and throwing its weight around, then it needs an attitude adjustment. Again, a sharp "no" and swift return to its cage might do the trick. On the other hand, the bird might want to return to its cage and has learned a quick method of getting back home. You need to be aware of patterns that develop: does your pet bite only when it's tired and wants to return to its cage? When your spouse comes near? (Could be a sign of jealousy.) When it's bored? (What better way to liven things up a little?) When you're not paying attention to it? (A sharp beak is a great attention-getting device.)

Once you've determined the triggers for a bite, you can begin to correct the behavior. Start by removing obvious triggers. For example, if your Quaker is jealous of another

Once you build a basic foundation of trust between you and your Quaker, you can train more complicated tricks and behaviors.

THE GUIDE TO OWNING A QUAKER PARROT

Aggressive biting is a problem, but owners should know the difference between a bite and when a bird uses its beak as a third foot to explore and test objects.

family member, try to give it extra attention when that person is around, before it bites you. If you do this consistently, the bird will begin to associate that person's presence with good things and will be less likely to bite. If it bites anyway, then punish it immediately with a sharp reprimand or return to its cage. Never, ever hit a bird! Not only can you cause serious injury, but you will destroy the parrot's trust in you and worsen its behavioral problems.

Resources

AFA Watchbird
American Federation of Aviculture, Inc.
P.O. Box 56218
Phoenix, AZ 85079
www.afa.birds.org

The AFA is a nonprofit organization dedicated to the promotion of aviculture and the conservation of avian wildlife through the encouragement of captive breeding programs, scientific research, and the education of the general public. The AFA publishes a bi-monthly magazine called *AFA Watchbird*.

Association of Avian Veterinarians
P.O. Box 811720
Boca Raton, FL 33481
561-393-8901
www.aav.org

AAV membership is comprised of veterinarians from private practice, zoos, universities and industry; veterinary educators, researchers and technicians; and veterinary students. Serves as resource for bird owners who are looking for certified avian veterinarians.

Bird Talk
Subscription Dept.
P.O. Box 57347
Boulder, CO 80323
www.animalnetwork.com

Bird Talk is a monthly magazine noted for its directory of avian breeders, as well as its species profiles and informative articles and columns on health care and behavior.

Bird Times
Pet Publishing, Inc.
7-L Dundas Circle
Greensboro, NC 27407
www.birdtimes.com

Bird Times is a source of entertaining and authoritative information about birds. Articles include bird breed profiles, medical reports, training advice, bird puzzles, and personal stories about special birds.

The Gabriel Foundation
P.O. Box 11477
Aspen, CO 81612
www.thegabrielfoundation.org

The Gabriel Foundation is a nonprofit organization promoting education, rescue, adoption, and sanctuary for parrots.

The NAPS Journal
North American Parrot Society, Inc.
P.O. Box 404
Salem, OH 44460
www.drzoolittle.com

NAPS members are individual pet owners, breeders with small and large aviaries, show judges, veterinarians, and people who enjoy exhibiting. Members can purchase closed bands from NAPS.

Midwest Avian Research Expo (MARE)
10430 Dewhurst Rd.
Elyria, OH 44035
www.mare-expo.org

MARE is a non-profit group dedicated to education and fund-raising for avian research projects.

Index

Photo Credits

Isabelle Francais:
pp. 11, 15, 27

Cindy Fredrick:
pp. 14B, 39, 49, 51, 60

Eric Ilasenko:
pp. 3, 7, 8, 9, 10, 14T, 17, 18, 19, 20, 22, 25TR, 30, 33, 36, 37, 44, 53, 57, 58

Horst Mayer:
pp. 45

Peter Rimsa:
pp. 6, 12, 13, 21, 23, 24, 25BL, 26, 28, 29, 35, 41, 43, 46, 47, 48, 50, 52, 54, 55, 59, 61

John Tyson:
pp. 1, 16, 34, 42, 56